From the cradle to college

Dedication

I would like to dedicate this work first to God and to him I give all honor and praise for blessing me with the gift of children, and my husband. Most of all, for salvation in Jesus Christ, which carries me daily.

I would like to say a sincere thank you to my loving and encouraging husband, without whom I wouldn't have finished this work

...and to my beautiful children whom God so graciously blessed me with in life. Thank you for your encouragement, your love and for the honor of being your mother. May these words bless your hearts all the days of your lives...

""...write the memories down, keep them and pass them forward"

Thoughts

I instantly fell in love with being a mother in 1992 but, I had no idea the roller coaster of emotion I had just boarded. My life would never be, just as yours will never be, the same. I experienced just as you will, joy, laughter, pride, heartbreak and moments of failure. There is no perfect mother or parent for that matter. The best we can do is strive to follow our own moral compass and embrace the power of prayer as we journey down the parenting road.

Sadly, the moments that will try your patients the most last only a short season. Somewhere inside of me I knew that time would pass swiftly and the little angels who filled my lap, my thoughts and my heart would be leaving me behind long before I would be ready to let them go.

I began journaling for many reasons. Most importantly was my wish to leave behind a gift for my children in my own penmanship, somewhat of an intimate gift in which I hoped my love for them would easily be felt over a vast amount of time.

In moments of weakness, when I felt the chaos was more than I could handle I found that God spoke to me, lifted and encouraged me to continue strong in my motherly duties.

I also recognized early being the mother of four that my memory would not serve me as well as I would hope. Hence, I felt writing their achievments, their thoughts and their words were well worth taking note of for the future, as well as my emotion in these moments.

I began a journal for each of my children. It is my hope to encourage mothers to do the same. I have been wrong about much in my life but these journals are by far one of the best things I have ever done. Now that my children are grown it is such a joy to read over these journals with them. So much would've been forgotten.

By tradition many mothers keep baby books but the journey goes so far beyond that brief infancy moment. Journaling your children's lives will give a continual life story. One that will encourage and even mend the broken heart you will endure at times while raising them.

The Lord also laid upon my heart many poems of different type about my children. I have included some in hopes that they will bring faith, encouragement and even laughter to you all. I pray you may all be blessed in the beautiful journey of motherhood. Embrace and hold tight, as it too will soon be a memory.

James 1:17

Every good and perfect gift is from above, coming down from the Father of the heavenly lights, who does not change like shifting shadows.

Rocking Chair

Little one please slow down
Please don't make me wear a frown
Stop now! Stop right there
Let us never leave this rocking chair

How I love your soft coo
Oh this love I feel is for only you
If you keep growing big and strong
One day little one, you'll be gone

Then all alone Ill be, just sitting here
An empty lap, In this rocking chair

Date:_____

Date:_____

Date:_____

Date:_____

Date:_____

Date:_____

Date:_____

Date:_____

Date:_____

Date:_____

Date:_____

YOUR'S

What have I done
surly not enough
Why has he blessed me with,
the warmth of your love

My ears hear your cries, yet they sing to my soul
My eyes see you lying there yet my heart cant believe

Not once or twice but blessed have I been,
three times and again

Many call you angels
God and I know far more
Your lives were a gift
Entrusted to me by the lord
God blew out a breath that whirled around the earth,
your soul trapped inside, as for me it did search

Then a spring breeze blew by my ear and in it
God whispered, I sent them to you dear

I made him a promise when I heard his voice
To love and guard you, punish and spoil,

Teach you morals from Gods word
To raise you always in the Lord

Date:_____

Date:_____

Date:_____

Date:_____

Date:_____

Date:_____

Date:_____

Date:_____

Date:_____

Date:_____

Date:_____

Flowers in bloom

A beautiful smile to brighten my day
A light in the night like a sun ray

Calmness is something I almost fear
Days of running laughing giggling and tears

Tattling and fighting sometimes drive me mad
But I know without them I would be terribly sad

They are my world, my very existence
I'd give life for them in an instant

Beautiful big eyes, little hands and pony tails
Hair cuts cars and little boats that sail

Trivial questions that never go away
Listening but not knowing what to say

Reading book after book
Baiting hook after hook

It's the good with the bad
And all that incures
But thinking of it all
Im quite reassured

That God's blessed me with angels here in my life
They make it all worth the struggle and strife

So I pray for the wisdom to stop and take a look
To write it all down in my memory like a book

For one day soon these precious ones will be gone
Ill look around then and find im alone

So ill stop and smell these flowers while their trying to bloom
For I know they'll be gone far far too soon

Date:_____

Date:_____

Date:_____

Date:_____

Date:_____

Date:_____

Date:_____

Date:_____

Date:_____

Date:_____

Date:_____

Home Interior

One day ago I attended a party of home interior
As to what beauties I'd see I wasn't quite sure

While I gazed at pictures, candles and frames
I could hear a lot of whispers and felt some shame

They all spoke of mirrors, flowers and glass
High prices, shelves, statues and brass

My budget was limited at none to spare
A purse that was empty, my pockets bare

The lady who spoke gave pointers and tips
Of how to decorate with flowers and give mirrors a flip

She intstructed of how to match all your frames

And I began to feel even more ashamed

When I left the party that night,
I dreamed of what owning those things would be like

When I walked through my door and looked around
The kids were in bed and there wasn't a sound

My mirror's reflections were surely not the best
And each frame was different from the rest

But sitting on my couch all alone
I realized my house could never be cloned

My décor was of great value and quite unique
All was happy and bold, really very neat

I had pictures of my children and family
There were shelves holding nic nacs of sweet memory

I saw a master piece made with Crayola
Splatter stains on a wall from a spilled coca cola

I also had decorations that couldn't be seen
they could only be felt if your senses were keen

In my home there was love to be shared
Happiness felt by a family who cared

Laughter was abundant and bounced off the walls
And the faint sound of tear drops from children so small

I smiled to myself and felt warm in my heart
Oh, that lady wasn't so smart

Within myself I was quite reassured
I knew I had the best,
HOME INTERIOR

Date:_____

Date:_____

Date:_____

Date:_____

Date:_____

Date:_____

Date:_____

Date:_____

Date:_____

Date:_____

Date:_____

Watch me

Watch me walk

Watch me talk

Watch me mommy, see me here

Watch me climb up in the chair

Watch me mommy while I eat

Watch me mommy while I sleep

Watch me mommy tie my shoes and ride my bike

Hear me, the red white and blue, recite

Watch me mommy sing and dance

Watch me mom take a chance

See me mom pick out my clothes

Did you see me mom, pierce my nose...

Watch me mom as I learn to love

See me cling to God above

Mom, watch and pray as I grow

Watch me break your heart real slow

Date:_____

Date:_____

Date:_____

Date:_____

Date:_____

Date:_____

Date:_____

Date:_____

Date:_____

Date:_____

Date:_____

What do elephants eat?

While sitting in our room trying to hide from the children,
My husband and I engaged in conversation
Trying to skim a hundred topics
before the moment would be stricken

just knowing that they were out there and would soon steal this time
we couldn't help but anticipate the conclusion of chit-chat,
his and mine

We weren't complaining, no not at all
for it wouldn't be long until they'd forget to even call

but we anticipated a wail from one or the other
an ouch or an argument over who gets the covers

maybe a sniffle, a cough or a hunger pain
or a tear from a movie horror scene

I lay there anxiously waiting for the thump of little feet
Conversation over, lights out
All was silent, except my heart beat

I grew dishearted, my spirit was diminished
as I thought,
So this is how I'll feel when their grown,
When we're finished

No one needed us, no little cries
No little hands curled up in mine

This emotion was not gloom or melancholy
There was no description, no words for how I felt, not any

Suddenly our door BURST OPEN and hit the wall, in
walked two children, one of which was quite small

The eldest just stood there and shrugged at me
The youngest said, "mommy can I ask you sumping?"

I was over joyed to see them standing at my bedside
My heart was jumping with joy, I felt happy inside

I quickly encouraged her question feeling sure
I would have an answer for it
As her mother and a fear diminisher,
I was quite well equipped

I was anticipating pulling her up in my arms,
Letting her fall asleep with me, assuring her of no harm.

As she climbed on my bed and had a seat...
She said, "mommy what do elephants eat?"

Date:_____

Date:_____

Date:_____

Date:_____

Date:_____

Date:_____

Date:_____

Date:_____

Date:_____

Date:_____

Date:_____

Blackeyed School Day

She is five years old
And off to kindergarten we go

She has her backpack, jacket and lunch,
"did I remember to pack it?"

Its her first day of school
She's so proud, she's so cool

She may be little and the baby of four
But she can handle herself she's tough to the core

As she let go of my hand, I began to cry
Then she turned and winked at me with her black eye

In that moment I dried up my tears
I knew she'd be fine...I had nothing to fear

Date:_____

Date:_____

Date:_____

Date:_____

Date:_____

Date:_____

Date:_____

Date:_____

Date:_____

Date:_____

Date:_____

Dear Lord...

Dear Lord,

How are you today? Much better than I, should I dare say.

I've been sitting here Lord all alone on my porch and I've the urge to write to you. It is burning now in my mind like a torch. I fear that I'm always busy, often too busy for you.

I have dishes to wash, children to tend, clothes in the dryer, bills to write...well you know, it never ends.

The chores that I have well, there so called blessings from you.

It all has to get done. What is it you expect from me? The chores are so many and the hours so few.

I have to get the girls ready each morning for school, feed them, dress them and brush their hair.

Then I get started with the baby and the four year old. Same things as before, should I list them all? Do you even care?

Of course I sweep and mop two to three times per week. I mean it's a new house you gave me and I have to keep it clean.

Then on to the bathrooms and laundry, which replenish themselves constantly.

When the phone rings I answer and listen to how his days going, then lay out something for dinner so it'll thaw entirely.

Then the baby needs a nap and I have to stop, sit down and rock her in my lap.

While I hold her, she likes for me to hum. I begin to wonder how I am ever going to get this all done.

I then look down at her golden curls, big blue eyes and dainty feet.

I start to remember other rocking hours with each of my children, they're all so unique.

I reflect on each of their lives and how wonderful they are. They shine all over my life and my memories. They are my personal little stars.

Lord, I'm sorry! I apologize for what I said. I wouldn't want to spend one night without them to tuck into bed.

The chores I complained about, well they aren't chores at all. They are extensions of true blessings that decorate within my walls.

I'm glad I wrote you this letter Lord and before I forget...

Thank you for loving me, blessing me and being with me each day, to you I am forever in debt.

Tired but blessed

Date:_____

Date:_____

Date:_____

Date:_____

Date:_____

Date:_____

Date:_____

Date:_____

*Date:*_____

Date:_____

Date:_____

The Game

As I was sitting in the bleachers last Saturday afternoon
The sun was blazing, my skin was melting and I looked like a prune
I asked myself this question about the role I was now playing,
"how did I get to be a baseball mom?", I mean I'm just saying.
I don't remember putting my parents through this as a child,
I know for a fact they never drove these miles
For the love of the game
My children sweat, ache and act insane
Hundred dollar uniforms, cleats and ball bags
Gloves, hats, helmets: the price of it all drives me mad
Five days a week I zig zag around
In three different directions at once I am bound
It's not even possible to be late with at least one
Because when it comes to playing the game,
I chauffer two girls and a SON
Monday through Friday they all have practice
But it's once the games start that I'm the saddest
Three schedules hang on the side of the frig

Three games on the same day and
The time difference isn't very big
I loose fifteen pounds each year during the spring
Running driving and sweating all to watch them play the game
I am not really sure just how I became a ball mom
This type of physical activity is something that as a child I ran from
But year after year I sit in these bleachers and yell
I scream each of their names until my breath is gone
And my face is pale
And as they step out of the dugout and into the batter's box
My chest swells and I'm the proud mom of a baseball jock
I realized something while sitting and sweating in those stands
I'm not just their mom, I'm their biggest fan

Date:_____

Date:_____

Date:_____

Date:_____

Date:_____

Date:_____

Date:_____

Date:_____

Date:_____

Date:_____

Date:_____

Angel on my tree

Angel angel on my tree
Please will you tell me what you see
Christmas day will soon be here
A time of happiness love and cheer
But Christmas in our house looks dim this year
My children are growing and soon will be gone
There will be no more Santa at the break of dawn
No toys to open and put together
No dolls, tea pots or indian feathers
Yet, you've reminded me that on Christmas day God sent his son
In a manger the holy savior was born
Then I stopped and thought of my four children and
The birth of my savior comes forward again
On Christmas night God sent his son
Mary gave birth knowing God's work had been done
Yet in a manger this mother rejoiced

Not as a must but as a choice
Oh what sadness she must have felt
Knowing the task this child had been dealt
If it weren't for God's loving pain
There would be no chance of heavenly life to gain
If without Jesus my children grow and become adults
With no salvation they'd endure death, life in hell, the last result
So angel on my tree show me more of what you've seen
That a babe was born on this holy night
To bare my children's sin, to win the fight
Because of this babe they'll grow big and strong
They'll make their choices between right and wrong
The blood he shed will cover them
And free them from their blame of their sin
Oh angel on my tree
Thank you for showing me
That on this holy night
My children's lives were in his sight

Date:_____

Date:_____

Date:_____

Date:_____

Date:_____

Date:_____

Date:_____

Date:_____

Date:_____

Date:_____

Date:_____

The day I met you

The day I met you I didn't know you, I saw water running down your eye,
It was running down mine as well who wiped it away, it was you
As I became two I sucked my thumb, who made it taste nasty, it was you
The day I went to kindergarten, who made me fit in, it was you
The day my boyfriend broke up with me who loved and comforted me
It was you
The day I fell and scraped my knee, who picked me up, it was you
The day it was my third birthday, who made me happy, it wasn't you
The day I made bad grades, who told me to try harder, it was you
Who bought me my dream horse, it was you
The day they were born, who gave me them to play with, it was you
The day I met you, who kissed me and said, i'll always be there for you
and love you, IT WAS YOU

I love you with all of my heart,
Pooh bear

Author's Note

The previous words were written as a gift for me on Mothers day by my eldest daughter. I kept this poem and have pulled it out over the years. She will never know what her written words put down personally for me mean as my journey goes forward.

Although my children are all grown now these moments, these emotions and these memories will always be a most treasured possession.

Remember to tuck away memories like this little poem from each child.

It will be more treasured than you can know...

Date:_____

Date:_____

Date:_____

Date:_____

Date:_____

Date:_____

*Date:*_____

Date:_____

Date:_____

Date:_____

Date:_____

Looking back

Looking back now through the years

It reddens my eyes to wipe the tears

As A child I loved you, even adored you at times

No one was like you, a rare find

It seems like a lifetime since I sat in your lap

Begging you, "mommy play with my hair while I take a nap"

I sure do miss the security of your arms

Being with you meant being safe from all harm

Isn't it funny how those feelings fade

Emotion of my childhood has been locked away

Then a little girl looked in my eyes

and said, "mommy come to my Halloween party please. Will you try?"

Then I remembered you working hard all week putting together for my Halloween party the cutest little treats

Then a second beautiful smile greeted me before bed

There was something troubling her, I could tell she was sad,

"mom will you tickle my back like when I was a kid, I want to be little for one night again.

That trigured emotions that I didn't know
I couldn't stop my tears, like a river they flowed
Suddenly I realized what I felt
It was not just sympathy for her but myself
I began to think...
Where had you gone? What happened to those years
Where was my safety net, my shield from my fears.
You had grown older and I was far too big for your lap
Now I am mother with chores and giving comforting naps
But oh what I wouldn't give to go back.

I wouldn't judge you like I did before,
You would never hear the slamming of my bedroom door
I'd stay with you when you were alone
And whenever you were leaving I'd beg you to stay home
I would treasure every moment that I had with you
Because now I know they are very few.
While all these thoughts were running through my head
I felt the tickling of two little hands
Suddenly, reality was staring at two little faces
And I realized that far too soon with them I would be trading places

I loved and adored you as a child

But as an adult you I admire.

Date:_____

Date:_____

Date:_____

Date:_____

Date:_____

Date:_____

Date:_____

Date:_____

Date:_____

Date:_____

Date:_____

The Journal

I have left you a gift, my family
A tangible gift full of love you see
Every time that you had a shining moment
Or crossed my mind, my fingers ran over it
I took pen in hand to write it all down
So one day you'll still have me when I'm not around
I'm sure to tell each one of you
That a million years are still too few
I write about the good and the bad
I write all the memories I have
It's important to me that you never feel alone
That while reading your journal you can still feel home

Made in the USA
Coppell, TX
28 September 2023